Myth Quest

Mahabali

THE GENEROUS ASURA

retold by Anu Kumar

illustrations by Amir Khan

First published in 2012 by Hachette India
(Registered name: Hachette Book Publishing India Pvt. Ltd)
An Hachette UK company
www.hachetteindia.com

SRD

ISBN 978-93-5009-536-2

Hachette Book Publishing India Pvt Ltd,
4th & 5th Floors, Corporate Centre;
Plot No. 94, Sector 44; Gurgaon 122003, India

Typeset in Adobe Garamond Pro 13/16
by Eleven Arts, New Delhi

Printed and bound in India by
Manipal Technologies Limited, Manipal

Welcome to the world of MythQuest…

Discover the fables and legends about the origin, history, deities, ancestors and heroes of India.

While the term 'myth' in common conversation means a false story, in the world of religion, folklore and magic, myths are considered 'true'. They tell stories of the creation of the universe, the eternal battle between good and evil and the history of humankind itself.

The main characters in our myths are bigger and better than any modern superheroes. They are birds and beasts, asuras *and gods, kings and queens, generals and warriors, sages and gurus, each with extraordinary powers that changed the course of history and the fate of the human race.*

The people to whom a myth belongs consider it as a true account of their past millions of years ago. Even today, they continue to worship the gods and goddesses, follow the rituals and read the texts that developed from these myths.

Hachette India's MythQuest series brings to you fascinating stories from the vast treasures of ancient mythology. Read them all—become a MythMaster!

Mythological characters and events have been described in different ways in different versions of ancient texts. We have chosen the most interesting and key stories to build a comprehensive account for the young reader.

This story is about . . .

The greatest of all asura *kings, Bali or Mahabali. He is also known as Maveli. Bali came from an illustrious line of powerful* asura *kings. He was the grandson of Prahlada and son of Virochana. His great-grandfather was the evil and much feared* asura, *Hiranyakashipu. All these* asuras *wreaked great evil in the world and usually met with disastrous ends at the hands of the gods.*

Despite being an asura, *Bali was a good and just king, known especially for his great generosity. His goal in life was to restore to the* asuras *their kingdoms and their dignity that they had lost to the gods. Bali was granted the boon of immortality by Brahma and spent years expanding his empire. He was invincible and conquered the three realms, Heaven, earth and the underworld. His kingdom was perfect in every way and his subjects loved him.*

Bali's story appears in the Vedas, in Buddhist and Jain literature, as well as the Ramayana as narrated by Vishwamitra.

Bali's generosity extended to humans and even impressed the gods. Lord Vishnu, the Preserver of the Universe, rewarded him for his benevolence by granting him a boon, whereby he could return to earth from the underworld once a year. During this time he could meet all his people. This occasion is marked as Onam in the state of Kerala.

Read Bali's exciting story as he traverses the three worlds, building a great asura *empire...*

CHAPTER ONE

A FAMILY OF CONTRASTS

A very long time ago, there lived two terrible but immensely powerful *asuras*, or demons. Their names were Hiranyaksha, meaning the one with the golden eyes, and Hiranyakashipu, meaning the one with the golden hair. For centuries, they had terrorized gods and men and were so powerful that it seemed no one could defeat them. Not satisfied with all the havoc they had caused in the three worlds, Hiranyaksha stole Prithvi, or earth, and held her captive under the raging and foaming cosmic ocean. The demon was ecstatic about his latest escapade. 'I am all-powerful,' he said. 'No god or mortal can challenge me now,' he roared in an awful voice that rang out through the universe. Little did he know that he was tempting fate and that the gods were listening to his empty boasts.

Soon enough, a great being would descend from Heaven and destroy him and his brother. This was no

other than Lord Vishnu, the Preserver of the Universe, who would take on various avatars to kill the *asura* brothers.

He took the form of Varaha, a boar, and descended into the depths of the sea to confront the evil *asura*. At first, Hiranyaksha was amused. 'Do you think a creature like you could defeat me, the greatest *asura* of them all?' he laughed. In reply, Varaha struck out with such divine force that Hiranyaksha fell back stunned.

Hiranyaksha quickly realized that he was in the presence of a powerful god and that it was no other than the invincible Lord Vishnu. However, for all his faults, the *asura* was brave and determined to fight till the end. They fought a bitter battle that lasted a thousand years. In the end, Hiranyaksha lay dead and the earth was lifted out of the water, borne on the tusks of Varaha.

Gods and men celebrated alike and the universe reverberated with the sounds of joyful celebrations. One creature, however, was far from joyous. This was the slain *asura's* enraged brother, Hiranyakashipu. He was consumed with grief and anger. 'I shall avenge my brother's death,' he promised.

His anger was terrible. He forbade the worship of Lord Vishnu throughout his kingdom. Lord Vishnu's images were defaced everywhere in his realm. He killed anyone who worshipped Lord Vishnu and mocked and abused him on every occasion.

In a strange twist of fate, Hiranyakashipu's son, Prahlada, ended up being a great devotee of Lord Vishnu. So great was the demon's hatred of Lord Vishnu that he was even willing to kill his own son! However, Lord Vishnu had promised to protect Prahlada. So now, he appeared in the form of Narasimha, a half-lion, half-man, and tore the evil *asura* apart. Prahlada was saved and was crowned the new king of the *asuras*.

Prahlada grew to be a great and wise king, much loved by all his subjects. And he remained an ardent devotee of Lord Vishnu all his life. Lord Vishnu, in turn, promised his protection to Prahlada and his descendants.

Thus Bali was born into such a family of contrasts. Born to Prahlada's son, Virochana and his wife Devamba, Bali grew up learning all about his famous and infamous ancestors. Bali's father, Virochana, himself was a learned scholar and a classmate of gods like Indra, who had studied under Prajapati, the ancient king of all creatures.

Prahlada doted on his grandson; Bali grew up in his grandfather's court with every attention lavished upon him. And even from a young age, he displayed his grandfather's traits of goodness, wisdom and kindness. Bali was brought up to be an ideal king. He learnt the virtues of good kingship and the principles of justice. He learnt the wisdom of the Vedas and other sacred texts from holy sages. He also learnt the art of warfare and the use of various weapons. In due course, he married Vindhyavali, the daughter of a saint.

As years passed, Bali grew more powerful and wonderful in every way. Even the three supreme gods, Lord Brahma, the Creator of the Universe, Lord Vishnu and Lord Shiva, the Great Destroyer, were pleased with him. He was soon acknowledged as the most powerful prince among *asuras*, and so he came to be known as Mahabali, or the Prince of Princes. Not only did he come from a family of mighty *asuras*, Bali himself was destined for greatness. Prahlada was now confident of his grandson's abilities. He knew that the *asuras* would be secure and safe under his rule. He thus decided to crown Bali as *yuvaraj,* or crown prince of the realm. However, Bali himself, was not ready to be *yuvraj*. He had bigger plans of his own.

CHAPTER TWO

A PRINCE, A GOD AND A BOON

Even as a very young prince, Bali had learnt one important truth. That the *devas*, or gods, and the *asuras* were always at war to rule the universe. In this war, sometimes the gods were victorious, sometimes the *asuras*. But the gods never lost an opportunity to humiliate and weaken the *asuras*. This knowledge would shape all of Bali's actions for the rest of his life.

There was one event in particular in which the gods clearly became superior and the *asuras*, weak. Cursed by a sage, the gods had lost their immortality and had asked Lord Vishnu to help them regain it. Vishnu told them to churn the Ocean of Milk to bring up the pot of *amrita,* or nectar which would make them immortal. Since they could not churn the ocean by themselves, the gods asked the *asuras* for help.

They placed the great mountain Mandara in the middle of the ocean. They coiled the magnificent serpent Vasuki around it. The *devas* held the tail end and the *asuras* held the end with the mouth. Together they churned the ocean for centuries. As they churned, many wondrous things came to the surface. Vile poisons also surfaced which Shiva swallowed. Finally, Dhanvantri, who would become the physician of the gods, emerged holding the pitcher containing the nectar of immortality.

With loud war cries, both the gods and *asuras* rushed to capture it. Virochana, Bali's father, was the first to grab it. He was about to escape with it, when sharp-eyed Garuda, Lord Vishnu's mount, swooped down upon him and plucked the pitcher out of his hands. Garuda lay the precious pitcher at the feet of Vishnu, who gave it to the gods. And thus they became immortal. The *asuras,* already weakened by years of conflict, became even weaker.

Bali had grown up hearing these stories and he had but one goal. He was determined that the *asuras* would regain their power and rule over the three worlds—the earth, Heaven and the underworld. 'Never again will the *asuras* be defeated by the *devas,* even if they possess the potion of immortality,' he vowed.

To achieve his goal, Bali knew he would need special powers. So when his grandfather announced his decision to make him the crown prince, Bali said to him, 'Sire, before I accept this great honour, I wish to gain greater power for the good of our people. Please allow me to leave your court to seek this boon from the gods.' Prahlada was sad to see his favoured child leave, but agreed.

And so Bali took leave of his family and left the grandeur of the court to live on top of a wild mountain. There he began to meditate. He prayed to Lord Brahma, Supreme God and Creator of the Universe because only Brahma had the power to decide where the balance of power lay, or who would rule supreme in the universe.

Decades passed and Bali meditated in the mountainous forests without food or water. So great was his will power and so intense was his concentration that he noticed nothing around him. The harsh sun beat down upon him; rain drenched

him; flakes of snow covered him in a blanket of white. But still Bali persevered in his penance.

Bali's prayers were very powerful. As his penance became more intense, dense clouds surrounded him. Flames shot up towards the sky. The gods, especially Lord Indra, were alarmed by the strength of Bali's prayers. Indra approached Brahma and said, 'O Lord and Creator of the Universe, Bali's penance will destroy the world. We beg you to make him end it.'

Brahma was deeply pleased with Bali's devotion and finally appeared before him. He sprinkled holy water on him and bade him to open his eyes.

'What is it that you want, O illustrious grandson of Prahlada?'

Bali knew he was already favoured as Prahlada's grandson. Prahlada was held in great esteem by the gods because of his loyalty and devotion to Vishnu, despite the taunts of his father, the wicked Hiranyakashipu.

Bali really did not want anything for himself. He wanted powers to help his people, the *asuras*. So he stood before Lord Brahma with his head bowed and humbly said, 'I ask for two things, O Divine Creator.'

Brahma nodded and waited for Bali to speak.

'I want to be immortal, so that I can always serve my people, the *asuras*. I want to always work for their happiness, always remain on the path of righteousness and ensure perfect justice for them.'

'And O Creator,' Bali went on, humbly bowing

low, 'Please grant me powers as great as Lord Indra, so that I stay undefeated in the cause of my people. May no evil enemy ever trouble my kingdom and my people.'

Brahma granted him his wishes, knowing that Bali would not misuse his gifts. Hearing this, the gods, especially Indra were dismayed. They were appalled that an *asura* was given the gift of immortality. They also believed that with his immense new powers, Bali would be invincible and create immense trouble for the gods.

They were however mistaken in this belief. Bali was a good and righteous being. His only intention was to be a just king and use his power for the good of his people. Now that Bali had what he wanted, he was ready for his responsibilities as a crown prince. So he hastened back to his capital where Prahlada was waiting for him.

CHAPTER THREE

THE RETURN OF THE PRINCE

The prince has returned! News of Bali's return spread like wildfire. The kingdom rejoiced as one. Every house was decorated with garlands of flowers and women painted decorative patterns on clay walls. Crowds lined the streets as Bali drove through the city in a magnificent chariot. The palace drummers stood on the ramparts and their drumbeats reverberated across the city as Bali entered the palace.

Prahlada was waiting to receive him. Embracing him, he said, 'It is time, my son, for you to take over the kingdom.' Bali bowed his head. 'Sire, the kingdom cannot do without your wise leadership. I beg you to remain king.' Prahlada reluctantly agreed. A few years later, however, he was able to persuade Bali to become the king. Even then, Bali ensured that his grandfather remained close at hand as his trusted adviser.

Bali's coronation was a grand affair. Once again, every home in the kingdom had been lavishly decorated. The city wore a freshly washed look and elephants and soldiers on horses lined the roads. Sages led by the venerated Shukracharya, chanted holy verses and prayers. 'O gods of Heaven and supreme beings of the

universe, we beg you to bless Bali's rule and make it the most benevolent in the entire universe,' they prayed.

Gods, demigods, *asura* kings and other kings from all over the world attended the ceremony. However, there was one god, Lord Indra, who could not overcome his jealousy and insecurity. And he refused to attend what was the grandest coronation ceremony on earth.

And thus began a golden era for the kingdom under the wise and just rule of Bali. Prahlada remained close at hand and the learned Shukracharya, the immortal holy sage, continued to serve as Bali's chief adviser.

Bali's subjects quickly learnt to love their new king. He treated them fairly and did not tax them too harshly. Above all, he gave the *asuras* the confidence and strength that they had lost over the ages. He opened his arms to brave warriors, learned scholars, artists and musicians who could not find a home anywhere. They began to forget their past humiliations and defeats and shone as precious gems in the court of Bali.

Next Bali amassed a large and loyal army. Bowing before his grandfather he said, 'Sire I wish to expand the kingdom and make the *asuras* all-powerful on earth.' Prahlada gave his blessings readily. However, he urged Bali to treat everyone kindly and even forgive those who had once opposed him.

'A wise king never makes lasting enemies of those he has conquered. Such an act is also an inspiration for his subjects. If his subjects see that he treats his defeated

enemies with graciousness, they will hold him in even higher esteem,' he advised.

And so Bali set out on his mission. He first turned his attention to his neighbouring kingdoms. The kings who ruled here were cruel and cared little for their subjects. They made them pay heavy taxes. Even in times of drought, they did nothing to help their people. As a result the people were miserable and the lands barren.

As Bali's army ventured further out, no one could stand in their way. Some kings held their ground and fought. But it was in vain. In no time at all, they fell to his superior strength. Others recognized his great power and surrendered without a fight, willingly accepting his sovereignty. They performed elaborate ceremonies, welcoming him and showering him with gifts and gold. Heeding his grandfather's advice, he treated his fallen enemies with respect. He allowed them to remain kings as long as they accepted his sovereignty.

Bali returned from his campaigns victorious and rich with wealth that other kings had showered on him. All the kingdoms as far as the eye could see were under Bali's rule—he was master on earth. But this was not enough. Bali wanted more. His main goal had always been to defeat the *devas*. So now, he now set his sights on the conquest of Heaven.

CHAPTER FOUR

THE STORMING OF HEAVEN

Bali assembled a large and powerful army and armed with an array of super weapons, they began their march towards Heaven. When the gods came to know of this, they quailed in alarm. 'Our forces are no match for his army!' they said. Bali's army was even more deadly because he led by example and every soldier in the *asura* king's army would lay down his life at a command.

Most of all, the news of Bali's advancing army alarmed Lord Indra, King of the Gods and Lord of Heaven. He knew that Bali himself was extremely powerful because of Brahma's boon. He also knew that he and the whole army of gods stood no chance against Bali. Obviously, being conquered by Bali's army would be very humiliating. And the thought of accepting Bali as his king was absolutely unacceptable In vain, he searched for a solution to his dilemma. Finally, he sought out Brihaspati, the guru and the spiritual adviser of the gods. 'O wise one, Bali is at the gates of Heaven. What must I do?' he asked.

The great sage replied, 'O king, you are the most powerful in Heaven but Bali is more powerful still. Despite being an *asura*, he is the fairest, most just king there ever was and nothing can stop him. His army will do his bidding, and even your army of gods realizes this. Leave your kingdom, hide in the forests, or other remote reaches of the universe and bide your time. It may be years, even longer, but one day, you will regain Heaven.'

Brihaspati was rarely wrong. So, Lord Indra swallowed his anger and his helplessness and rode away with the gods.

A few days later, Bali entered the gates of Heaven unopposed and found that Heaven had no king! Needless to say, he had won an easy victory.

However, Bali was a large-hearted king. He did not crow in triumph, or gloat over how easily the gods had given up. Instead, he ensured that Heaven was set in order. He placed his trusted men in responsible positions, reassured the few demigods and other beings

that still remained there, that he meant no harm and having made sure that things would run smoothly in Heaven, he returned in triumph to his kingdom.

The conquest of Heaven was celebrated with great joy. Bali had done the unthinkable—he had driven away the gods from Heaven and restored to the *asuras* their long lost pride. And all of this had been carried out without any bloodshed.

CHAPTER FIVE

THE MIGHTY KING AND HIS GREAT SACRIFICES

Bali returned victorious. His subjects celebrated and his courtiers sang his praises. But Bali was not content. He addressed his adviser, the guru of the *asuras*, Shukracharya.

'O guru, I have gained immense wealth and it will last me several generations. I would like to use it for the benefit of my people. Pray tell me, how I can do that?'

Shukracharya was very pleased with Bali's generous views. He smiled and said, 'You are now the master of three worlds; thus you have an even greater responsibility towards your subjects. And it is true O king, that this wealth belongs to all your subjects, for it is their hard work that has made your kingdom prosperous. So it is only right for you to share your wealth with them.'

Shukracharya advised Bali to distribute the wealth equally amongst his people. 'This will also ease the suffering of the poor and there will be absolute justice and peace in the kingdom. Now is the time to cement your position as one of the greatest rulers in all the three worlds,' advised the sage.

'How shall I do that, O sage?' asked Bali.

'You must perform the Vishwajit Sacrifice,' said Shukracharya. 'This sacrifice literally means to win the world and after performing it successfully you will be the undisputed ruler of the three worlds.'

The Vishwajit was a massive sacrifice and news that Bali was going to perform it was greeted by awe in many quarters of the universe. Among the gods, however, there was great consternation.

The gods could not believe it. They thought Bali's ambition seemed to have no bounds and even ruling over Heaven wasn't enough for him.

But none of this made any difference to Bali as he was determined to carry out his guru's wishes. The kingdom he ruled over, must be the most perfect one that ever existed. The ceremony was lavishly organized and conducted in a proper manner and it did add to the fame of this great king.

Bali thereafter devoted himself to the duties of kingship.

He travelled to all parts of the empire to see for himself how his people lived. He advised the *asuras* to live wisely and well, and never stray from the right and honest path. Only then, he told them, would they be as widely respected as the gods.

Bali also held open court sessions, where people could come and air their grievances. He was generous, kind and ever-patient. He helped farmers and merchants, and ensured that there was peace, law and order in every corner of his empire.

Naturally, such an ideal state of affairs could not last for long. Lord Indra, who was most unhappy in his exile, could not contain his jealousy any further. He now began to look for an opportunity to return to his rightful place.

Shukracharya knew that the gods would never rest easy, having lost their kingdom to Bali. So, now he advised Bali to perform a hundred Ashvemadha sacrifices. Thus his power would be secure. In this sacrifice, Bali's horse, followed by his army, would roam throughout the lands. If the horse was stopped by a king, it meant that the king was challenging Bali and would have to fight his army. If the horse was allowed to pass through unchecked, this meant that the king of that region accepted Bali's supremacy.

Shukracharya chose the holy city of Bhrigukacha, on the banks of the river Narmada as the site for the sacrifices. This was an ancient thriving port, from where ships of distant places visited and where rich merchants had their posts.

Ninety-nine times the sacrifice was performed. Ninety-nine times the royal horse rode free through different kingdoms with Bali's huge army behind him—no one stopped or challenged him. Bali's sacrifices left no king in doubt that he was the most powerful ruler in the universe. Once the hundredth sacrifice would be held, Bali would be invincible.

News of this sacrifice spread rapidly across the land and in no time at all reached the ears of Lord Indra in his hideout. When Lord Indra heard about this second supreme sacrifice, he couldn't control himself any longer. He was consumed by a wild and terrifying jealousy. How could anyone else become so powerful, when he, Indra, King of Gods, had to live the life of a refugee? He decided that Bali not only had to be defeated, he had to be humiliated and deprived of all that he had gained! It was now time to dislodge Bali and regain his power in Heaven before it was too late.

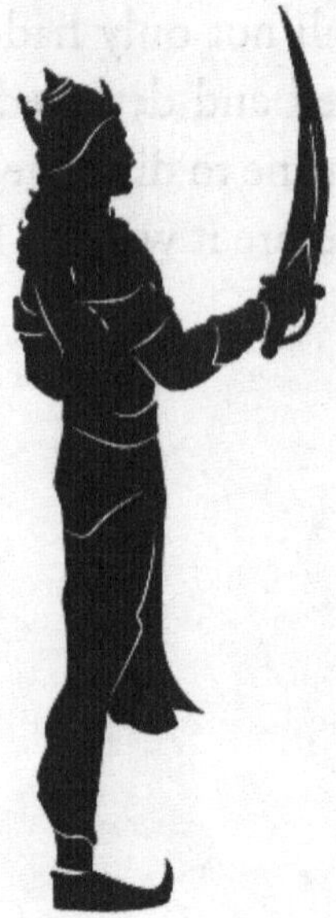

CHAPTER SIX

A JEALOUS GOD AND A BOON

Indra summoned Kalipurush, the spirit of all evil things. Kalipurush was a creature that thrived on creating misery and wretchedness all around him. He was sickly and ragged with folds of loose flesh hanging from his bony frame. His hair was matted and straggly and he was without doubt, the ugliest creature one ever saw. He was ever loyal to Indra's every command and appeared the moment Indra thought of him.

'What do you see in Bali's kingdom?' the King of the Gods commanded.

Kalipurush closed his eyes. Then he frowned and

replied, 'I see prosperity everywhere, O king. Bali's subjects are very happy under his rule. They have nothing to complain about. Bali takes care of them . . .'

Stung by this praise, Indra interrupted him angrily, 'I didn't summon you to sing Bali's praises. I want you to go at once to Bali's kingdom and spread your misery. Stop the seeds from growing, make the trees wither away, set fire to standing crops, make the rivers run dry. Do your worst, so that Bali's subjects will soon begin to hate him.'

Kalipurush went to Bali's kingdom and did as he was commanded. He caused famine in parts of the kingdom, but Bali quickly ordered his men to move supplies of grain to the affected parts. He ordered canals dug and taxes were waived, and so no one suffered. Kalipurush then started forest fires across vast areas, but Bali himself toured the affected villages and was generous with his help.

Defeated, Kalipurush returned to Lord Indra. 'O Lord, I have failed. Bali is truly invincible because he has the love of his people. There is nothing he cannot do.'

Obviously, Indra was extremely annoyed with Kalipurush's failure. But he was still obsessed by his desire to see Bali ousted.

He now sought his mother, Aditi, who lived on Mount Meru with her husband, the wise sage Kashyapa. Kashyapa and Aditi were parents to all the gods. Indra narrated his story to Aditi and she became deeply distressed to see Indra and all her children so unhappy.

'Let us go to Lord Brahma,' she said. 'After all it was he who gave Bali his powers.' And so Aditi, Kashyapa and Lord Indra made their way to Lord Brahma's abode.

'O Supreme Lord,' said Kashyapa. 'You are the Creator and make things possible. Do you not see how unfair it is—that an *asura* should rule all the three realms while the gods skulk in fear? After all, in the natural order of things, it is the gods who should actually rule Heaven.'

Lord Brahma shook his head, 'I am only the Creator. I cannot help you. Lord Vishnu can help you—he is the Preserver and the one who restores the rightful balance and the order of things in the universe.'

And so he advised Kashyapa and Aditi to propitiate Lord Vishnu. 'I am sure he will listen to your prayers, even though he has promised his protection to Prahlada and his descendants.'

Aditi and Kashyapa began their meditation. They spent years in penance. Lord Vishnu of course was omniscient and all-knowing. When he saw that Aditi, mother of the gods, was pleading for his help, he hastened to appear before her.

'O Gracious Mother, since you have summoned me, something must be causing you great worry. Rest assured, I shall grant whatever it is that you wish.'

'O Supreme Lord, my children, the gods have had to flee their homes in fear of Bali. My son Indra and others are homeless while Bali rules in Heaven. Is this fair? I beg you to intervene and restore the balance of power,' Aditi beseeched.

Lord Vishnu nodded in agreement. However, he listed his problems. 'First there is my promise to Prahlada, my most loyal devotee, that I will always protect his descendants. Second, even though he is an *asura*, Bali is a most righteous and fair king and his subjects truly love him.'

'So...' Lord Vishnu told Aditi, 'If the gods have to

return to Heaven, Bali will have to be defeated by very unusual means. He cannot be summoned to battle, or engaged in a duel. He cannot be killed by deception, for there is no other king as fair and just as he is. He can only be defeated if he makes a mistake on his part. A mistake that will be a result of his own innate goodness.'

Lord Vishnu then left Aditi with a promise, 'When it becomes imperative, I will appear in the dwarf, or the Vamana avatar and Bali shall commit a fateful mistake. And this will bring back to the universe the balance that existed even before time did.'

Aditi was relieved and reassured. She returned to her sons and told them to be patient. Lord Vishnu would intervene when the time was ripe.

CHAPTER SEVEN

PRAHLADA'S ADVICE

Meanwhile in Bhrigukacha, Bali was preparing to perform the hundredth sacrifice, as advised by his guru. With this sacrifice completed, Bali would become the most powerful king in the universe. There would be simply no one left to challenge him.

Bali's kingdom had been near perfect due to his own good governance and generosity. However, unknown to Bali, there was a growing unrest in some parts of the kingdom. Within the realm, some *asura* rulers had become increasingly arrogant. They realized that they enjoyed great power and had began to abuse it. They began to bully and oppress the people. When the people opposed them or protested, the *asuras* taunted in return,

'Bali, the greatest of *asura* kings is now the king of the universe. There is no one who you can go to for help now.' Their cruel laughter struck terror in the hearts of the people.

This state of affairs soon came to the notice of Bali's grandfather, Prahlada. Though he was now very old, Bali doted on him and frequently sought his advice. Hearing about how reckless and arrogant the *asuras* had become, he summoned Bali and informed him about this. Prahlada was an astute and far-sighted elder and he realized that Bali's hard work to elevate the *asuras* could all be doomed if such reports continued.

'This sacrifice you are so keen to perform, will give the *asuras* powers they don't really deserve. Mark my words, when ambition oversteps its limits, the supreme and all-powerful gods step in to curtail it. You must be careful.'

But Bali, who had so far listened to every word that Prahlada had said to him, now demurred. He had performed ninety-nine sacrifices and remained unchallenged, and believing that such a trend would continue, he ignored his grandfather's well-chosen words for the first time. Instead he said, 'Everything has been planned, Sire. Gurudeva awaits your presence, and I have come to fetch you.'

Prahlada was offended by this dismissal of his warnings. This time he warned Bali so sternly, it almost sounded like a curse.

'Be careful. Lord Vishnu sees everything, everywhere and he will soon appear if your arrogance and those of the *asuras* you lead knows no bounds. One day, if you go too far, you will lose this kingdom that you have so painstakingly acquired and find yourself exiled from earth forever.'

Bali paled and regretted his behaviour instantly. He begged his grandfather for forgiveness. Prahlada too was contrite at his over harsh words. In a softer tone he said, 'Lord Vishnu is all forgiving. He is also just. He will never fail you if you repent your ways.'

With these last words of advice, he accompanied his grandson to the sacrificial hall.

CHAPTER EIGHT

A SMALL MAN TAKES A VERY LARGE STEP

The sacrificial hall was immense and even from a distance, strains of music and the melodious chants of more than a thousand priests could be heard. Shukracharya sat at the centre of them all, pouring holy oblations into the fire. The fire rose higher and higher, casting a bright orange glow over hall. Mahabali, swathed in a gold-threaded cloak, sat with his wife Vindhyavali by his side. Shukracharya paid special attention to the rituals. It was the hundredth sacrifice and he wanted nothing to go wrong.

The rituals reached their climax and the incantation of the sages rose high up to the sky. Bali, however,

noticed that Shukracharya wore a worried frown on his face. He leaned forward and asked the sage, 'O blessed one, is there something that worries you?'

'O king, now that the rituals are complete, it is time for you to make your gifts. You have promised to give everybody everything they ask for. But mark my words, I sense that the gods are now more worried than before. They might try to trick you in some way and regain their power,' said the sage.

Bali was now at the height of his powers and this gave him great confidence. The culmination of this sacrifice would place him higher than any being in the universe. He dismissed his guru's advice in the same way that he did Prahlada's. 'I don't think anyone would dare trick me so openly and especially today of all days!'

But Shukracharya shook his wise old head. 'You do not know Lord Indra and the gods. And if they have asked Lord Vishnu himself to step in, that will make things very difficult for you, for Lord Vishnu has a way out for everything. O King, I beg you, be careful. Do not make rash promises. Be generous, but also be cautious about what you give away.'

Bali tried not to show his displeasure, but he did not like the sage's advice. 'I will try to do as you advise. However, when the history of the universe is narrated, I would like to be remembered as a truly selfless and generous king. I have heard legends of kings and sages of yore, who even gave away their bodies when someone begged it of them. I would like to believe I am no less. In this way, I will win the gratitude of my people, and the blessings of the supreme gods for all time.'

Even as Shukracharya and Bali conversed, a soft murmur rippled through the crowds. Bali raised his head and saw the crowd part like a river to make way for someone. It was the smallest human being he had ever seen. He was a dwarf. Yet, the dwarf carried himself with a dignity that would have suited a much older and taller sage. He carried an umbrella, and was dressed simply in a loose cloth that reached down to his knees. He had a small round face, markings in sandalwood paste on his forehead, and a serious expression that belied his youth. The young sage bowed low before Bali, Shukracharya and Queen Vindyavali.

'O king, blessed is anyone who is ruled and protected by a king as generous and benevolent as you are.'

Bali bowed his head and waited for the tiny Brahmin to speak.

'I have come from far away, hearing of this sacrifice—the most magnificent and grand sacrifice ever performed by a king. And I have heard of your generosity too, it is something that would put even the King of Gods to shame. But O king, I don't have much to ask for.'

Shukracharya felt the first stirrings of disquiet, but Bali would not look his way. The compliments pleased him immensely. He smiled widely and replied in turn. 'Do not hesitate to ask for what you desire, O young *vamana*. It will be my honour to serve you.'

He invited the young sage to be seated on a magnificent velvet couch and asked him what he wanted. 'A gift,' the *vamana* said. 'But I hope it won't be too much for you.'

Bali suppressed a smile, while a wave of laughter swept through the audience. Only Shukracharya was not amused. He was aware of an impending sense of doom.

'I am sure I can fulfil any request you have, O learned young sage,' the king assured him. 'Ask me anything and

I will do my best. Land, jewels, forests—your word is my command.'

The *vamana* hesitated. He looked around, almost as if he was embarrassed by what he was going to demand. The king waited, as did everyone else, the atmosphere pregnant with an expectant silence.

The *vamana* spoke up, 'You have never denied anyone anything. Isn't that true?'

The king nodded and his courtiers did the same. Only wise Shukracharya stood silent, his frown still marked. 'And once you make your promise, you do not retract it. I've heard that too.'

The king repeated what he had said before, 'O holy sage. You sound wise beyond your years. I can assure you that no one who has asked for anything from me has gone back disappointed.'

The sage spoke up again, 'I am Vamana, son of Kashyapa. I do not need great wealth, or much of your vast kingdom. I need just enough to pay my *gurudakshina,* or gift to my guru, Bharadwaj.' He continued in a low, shy voice. 'My teacher does not require much. All I ask for him are three paces of land. As much land as I can measure with three paces of my feet.'

There was a sudden silence. No one could believe their ears. This was not what they had expected to hear. Three paces of land was far too less, and when measured by the small feet of the vamana, it was a near ridiculous request!

'Are you sure?' The king asked.

Vamana nodded, 'I am. That is what I want. Do you think, O king, that you can fulfil your promise?'

This time Shukracharya could not hold himself back. 'Oh king, don't make this promise. I am sure you will repent it.'

Bali smiled. This could not be a test of his famed generosity! 'I cannot refuse your request. You are welcome to measure the land you need for yourself.'

'Thank you, O king' said the young sage with great dignity, as he stood up.

He stepped down from the podium. Then he walked out into the open field, where he would measure out the land he would need.

Everyone watched with bated breath. They had no idea of what would happen next.

Vamana drew a deep breath, and then to everyone's amazement, he started to grow in size. He grew taller and taller. His feet and limbs stretched longer and longer, as he shot higher. It was then that Shukracharya spoke up. He said gravely, with sadness in his voice. 'O king, Vamana is none other than Lord Vishnu. He is here in this incarnation to humiliate you and to make you lose all that you have gained so far.'

Bali had already realized that the dwarf growing before his eyes could be no ordinary creature. He had to be someone divine, with great powers. But as he had already made a promise, he was sworn to grant Vamana his three paces of land.

Vamana had grown bigger than a tree, and then within seconds, he was taller than a giant and the people had to crane their necks to look at him. His head broke through the clouds, and the crowds fled in terror as his feet grew larger than a mountain.

Then in a deep and ancient voice, he spoke. 'And now I take my first step.' He raised his foot, and huge shadow fell on the earth cast by the length of his foot. Humans and all other creatures cried out for fear of being trampled upon, but the Vamana did not set his foot upon his earth. He stood, his foot hovering over the earth, and said, 'I claim the earth with my first step. O king keep your word and grant me the earth.' Bali bowed low and nodded. He watched as the giant took another step. His foot rose high and stretched across the vast blue skies like an infinitely growing snake, till they could see it no more. Vamana's deep voice was once more heard from the vastness of the sky. 'O king, I have covered Heaven with my other foot. Grant me Heaven and be a man of your word.' Bali said quietly, accepting the inevitable, 'Yes, I give away two paces of land to you, O Vamana.'

And the great voice still boomed from above. 'Where will I get my third and last pace of land from, O king? I cannot see any more land. Have you truly lost everything?' There was a mocking note in his voice, and Bali, drawing himself up to his full height, looking up as far as he could, said with all the kingly dignity at his command, 'Place it on my head, O Vamana, as there is no other place for you to place your last step.'

This humble gesture and Bali's humiliation greatly angered the *asuras*. They saw that their beloved king had been deceived. It was an elaborate trick carried out by Lord Vishnu to save the gods. Bali stood there, looking small and beaten as Vamana's foot hovered over him. All his *asura* soldiers rushed towards the giant and stood armed with spears, ready to unleash their arrows, only waiting for a word of command from their king.

Bali looked at them as he knelt under Vamana's foot. 'This is indeed the great Lord Vishnu. He is Vamana and now in this giant form, he is also Trivikram. I am honoured to be able to pay my obeisance to him. No sacrifice is too great if Lord Vishnu demands it and I am honoured that he has chosen me to make his demand.' Bali also told the *asuras*. 'Lord Vishnu cannot be vanquished and he is on the side of the gods, so they have won back what we conquered from them.'

He felt Vamana's foot on his head and then he felt himself sinking into the soft earth towards the realm called the underworld. As Bali sank into the earth, he heard his subjects wailing in grief. Bali after all was a much-loved king. His subjects wept to see him like this—not just defeated but also humiliated. Much later, it was this insult to his father that would make Banasura, Bali's thousand-armed son, Lord Vishnu's arch-enemy.

Bali heard the piteous wailing and hastened to comfort his subjects. 'Do not weep, O *asuras*. I made Vamana a promise and I am duty bound to keep my word. I have to give him space to place his third pace. I cannot break my promise. This is a lesson to all *asuras* not to become too proud and arrogant; they will pay the price for it. That is what my grandfather tried to tell me, but I did not heed his words.'

As Vamana heard Bali's advice to his fellow *asuras*, he spoke again from his great height, 'Bali, you are indeed the greatest king of all. Not only are you immortal, but you are also a generous and just king. For this, I crown you the king of *Sutala,* or the underworld. And I promise to protect your realm just as I had once given my word to your grandfather.'

Bali bowed his head and he felt the soft pressure of Vishnu's foot as he began to sink into the earth. As he saw himself moving into a new world of darkness inhabited by strange looking creatures, who were never seen on the surface of the earth, he folded his hands in resignation.

'O king, I grant you one last boon. Ask of me what you desire,' said Vamana.

Bali saw his very distressed subjects and said, 'O Lord, every year, I would visit my subjects to see to their well-being, first hand. There isn't a single part of my kingdom I did not visit at least once a year. I will continue to think of my subjects in my underworld home. And every year, just like I always did as their king, I wish to be allowed to visit them.'

Vamana granted him this boon before Bali disappeared into *Sutala*. The gods led by Lord Indra returned triumphant to Heaven amidst the sounds of celebration.

But in Bali's kingdom, the only sounds heard were of weeping and wailing, as people mourned the loss of their much-loved king.

However, as Vishnu had decreed, Bali returned every monsoon to visit his people, for which they prepared for days in advance and even after hundreds of years passed, Bali continued to be remembered and loved in the land he had once ruled with such benevolence.

MythNotes

Even today, the return of Bali is celebrated in Kerala as the festival of Onam. It is believed that on this day, Bali revisits his subjects on earth. The day of Bali's return is marked by immense gaiety. The harvest has been gathered and there are joyous celebrations, including boat races, where rowers in long snake boats race each other for the victory spoils. Everyone wears new clothes; even houses wear a fresh new coat of paint. Seven forts are made of clay, or cow dung and this is where the king is symbolically welcomed and worshipped. At night, lamps are lit everywhere to welcome the king for his day-long visit to earth.

In the sacred literature of the Jains, there is another story relating to the claiming of three paces of land. There was once a king called Mahapadma of Hastinapura and he had a minister called Namuci. Namuci harassed and greatly troubled the Jain sages and monks in Hastinapura. So the Jain monks appealed to the holy sage Vishnu to intervene on their behalf. Vishnu asked the minister for three paces of land so the monks could build a monastery there to live peacefully. The minister agreed, but most reluctantly. Then Vishnu swelled in size and he placed his right foot on Mount Mandara. Another account in the Harivamsapurana, says that Vishnu the sage took three paces, and stepped on two of Heaven's foremost peaks Mandara, Manasottara and then stood on Heaven itself—thereby claiming the entire universe for himself.